STAR FINDER

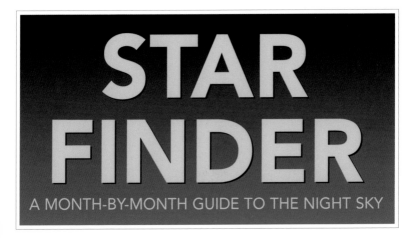

STAR FINDER

A MONTH-BY-MONTH GUIDE TO THE NIGHT SKY

JOHN WOODRUFF AND WIL TIRION

THUNDER BAY
P · R · E · S · S
San Diego, California

Thunder Bay Press
An imprint of the Advantage Publishers Group
5880 Oberlin Drive, San Diego, CA 92121-4794
www.thunderbaybooks.com

© Philip's 2000, 2003

Reprinted 2006

All notations of errors or omissions should be addressed to
Thunder Bay Press, Editorial Department, at the above
address. All other correspondence (author inquiries,
permissions) concerning the content of this book should
be addressed to Philip's, a division of Octopus Publishing
Group Ltd, 2–4 Heron Quays, London E14 4JP, U.K.

ISBN-13: 978-1-59223-089-1
ISBN-10: 1-59223-089-X

Printed in China.

5 6 7 8 9 09 08 07 06 05

Text   John Woodruff

Star charts   Wil Tirion

Moon photographs (pp24–25) © UCO/Lick Observatory

Contents

The Night Sky

Nature has fewer sights more spectacular than the night sky. On a clear moonless night, even from an urban location, hundreds of stars may be visible. Away from towns and sources of artificial light the spectacle is awesome. The number swells to thousands: seemingly countless stars sparkling against the jet-black depths of space, like brilliant jewels on a velvet backcloth. At first glance the distribution of stars seems random. Look a little longer, and some order emerges – here and there some of the brighter stars form themselves into distinctive patterns. (Some of these patterns can be easier to pick out when fewer stars are visible.) From ancient times, watchers of the sky have sought such patterns among all the stars they could see. These patterns, modified and augmented in more recent times, form the system of *constellations* in use today as a convenient way of locating positions in the night sky.

This book provides the first-time stargazer with a clear and straightforward guide to viewing the stars and constellations on show over the course of the year. The only requirements are reasonable eyesight and a clear sky. The best way to become familiar with the stars is to use what astronomers call the naked eye. Binoculars or a telescope will reveal some spectacular sights. But the best way to get to know the night sky is with your eyes alone.

Stars in Motion

One of the first things that is noticeable about the night sky is that the stars do not move relative to one another. The patterns visible on one night will still be there a week or a year later. (A star-like point that is moving will be an artificial satellite. One that shifts position over the course of weeks or months will be a planet – see page 22.) But, as will become clear after half an hour or so, the whole panoply of stars itself appears to rotate about a fixed point, as if they were on the inside of a giant umbrella, and you were slowly turning the shaft.

Just as the Sun appears to move across the daytime sky, this apparent motion of the stars is a result of the Earth rotating on its axis. The point about which the stars appear to rotate is called the *north celestial pole*. Fortunately it is marked by a fairly bright star, appropriately named Polaris, which is easy to find (see page 13) and provides a simple means of direction-finding: if you are facing Polaris, you are facing north. All the other stars appear to be moving on circular paths around

Polaris. The farther they are from Polaris, the larger the circles they trace out. A long-exposure photograph made by pointing a camera at the north celestial pole for several hours shows the 'trails' of stars as a series of concentric arcs (not full circles, for there are not 24 hours of darkness).

The angle Polaris makes with the horizon (called its *altitude*) is the same as your latitude. If you are observing from London (latitude 51½°N), the altitude of Polaris is 51½° – just over halfway from the horizon to the point overhead, called the *zenith*. From any location on Earth between the equator and the poles, the circular paths of the stars are inclined to the horizon – as if the point of the imaginary umbrella were aimed diagonally upwards. Over the course of a night, stars rise at the eastern horizon (just as the Sun does), climb the sky towards the south, then descend to the western horizon, where they set. Which stars are on view thus depends on the time of night.

From any given latitude, some stars are visible throughout the night. If a star's angular distance* from the north celestial pole is less than the altitude of Polaris, it can never set. Such stars are called *circumpolar* (see page 13). From latitudes of just over 40°, for example, the familiar grouping known as the Plough or Big Dipper, used to locate Polaris, is circumpolar. Similarly, there will always be stars permanently out of view. For northern-hemisphere observers, any star whose angular distance from the south celestial pole is less than their latitude can never rise.

Seasonal Changes

So, some stars never set while others never rise. For the others, it is not only the time of night that determines whether they will be on view, but also the time of year. For example, the constellations that mark the winter sky are not seen in the summer months. To understand why this should be, it is necessary to look at the Earth's rotation on its axis and its orbit around the Sun. The Earth spins on its axis in about 23 hours and 56 minutes. This, the time it takes to return to the same position relative to the stars, is four minutes shorter than the solar day of 24 hours used for timekeeping. The solar day is the time it takes the Earth to return to the same position relative to the Sun. After one complete rotation, it has to turn a little further on its axis to do this, because it has travelled a little further in its orbit. This difference means that, in terms of our 24-hour clock, any one star will rise four minutes earlier than on the previous night, or two hours earlier each month. After 12 months, the Earth has completed one orbit of the Sun, the two

clocks are back in step, and the stars are back to their same times of rising.

This combined effect of the daily and annual changes in the night sky is reflected in the monthly charts on pages 26–49. The January chart, for example, shows the stars visible on 5 January at 11 p.m. or 21 January at 10 p.m., but also on 21 December at midnight, 6 December at 1 a.m., 5 February at 9 p.m., 20 February at 8 p.m., and for correspondingly later times at earlier dates, and earlier times at later dates (for times which are hours of darkness). When daylight saving time is in operation, subtract an hour from the times given. The striking winter constellation Orion illustrates the seasonal variations in the sky. The January chart shows how it dominates the southern winter sky. By 10–11 p.m. in March Orion is about to set, and does not reappear on the charts until October, when it is rising in the east at around this time.

Constellations

The 88 modern constellations (see page 19) between them cover the whole of the sky. Just over half of them are of ancient origin, and bear the names of people, creatures and objects, mostly from ancient legends. The rest were added from the 16th to the 18th century, to fill the uncharted southern skies and the gaps between the northern constellations occupied by faint stars. The brighter stars also have names. Many of them derive originally from medieval Arab astronomy, but some have become so corrupted over time that they no longer mean anything in Arabic.

* It is convenient to measure the separation between two points in the sky as an angle. So, for example, the distance from the zenith to the horizon is 90°. In the same way the Moon is said to have a diameter of ½°.

Constellations vary considerably in size and prominence. A few, such as Orion, are unmistakable. Some may be picked out quite easily, while others, even on a very clear night, are very faint and hard to identify. The minor constellations are omitted from the monthly charts on pages 26–49, but are included on the main charts (pages 13–18).

Some prominent groupings of stars are not constellations in their own right, but form part of a larger one. The brightest of these *asterisms*, including the Plough (part of Ursa Major, the Great Bear) and the Square of Pegasus, are labelled on the charts.

The ancient astronomers who framed the constellations did not appreciate that stars which appear to be closely grouped in the sky almost always have no association with one another. What look like distinctive triangles, chains and other configurations are invariably made up from stars which lie at very different distances. Their apparent connection is a result of chance: our lines of sight to these stars happen to lie close together. There are exceptions, though. Most of the stars of the Plough, for example, are moving through space together. And some stars reside in *clusters* – collections of dozens or even thousands of stars closely packed together. The Pleiades (page 54) is a cluster close enough for its individual members to be visible.

Star Brightnesses

The stars we see in the night sky differ in brightness for two reasons: they lie at different distances from one another, and some are intrinsically more luminous than others. A star's brightness is reckoned according to a scale of *magnitudes* that originated in ancient times. The brightest stars were said to be of first magnitude, those not quite so bright of second magnitude, and so on down to the faintest stars visible, which were sixth magnitude. (The lower the magnitude value, the brighter the star.)

Nowadays the magnitude scale has been put on a proper mathematical footing, and extended to magnitude zero and to negative values for the brightest objects, and to seventh magnitude and beyond for the myriad fainter objects visible in telescopes. Accurate measurements make it possible to quote values to two decimal places. The brightest star, Sirius, has a quoted magnitude of −1.44. A star of magnitude 1.0 is by definition a hundred times as bright as one of magnitude 6.0. A magnitude difference of exactly one corresponds to a difference in brightness of just over 2½. 'First magnitude' means a star between magnitudes 0.5 and 1.5, 'second magnitude' between 1.5 and 2.5, and so on. The monthly charts (pages 26–49) show all stars down to third magnitude, together with fourth-magnitude stars which help to make up some of the fainter constellation patterns. The main charts show all stars down to approximately magnitude 5.0. Some stars are variable – their brightness fluctuates instead of remaining steady (see page 52). Some important variable stars are shown on the charts as a white ring rather than a solid disk.

Although the stars appear white at first glance, the colours of the brightest ones will soon become apparent. A star's colour is an indication of its surface temperature. The coolest stars shine with a red light ('cool' is relative – red stars have a surface temperature of around 3000°C). Orange, yellow, white and blue represent progressively higher surface temperatures. The brightest stars have their colours shown on the charts. Fainter stars are perceived as white for physiological reasons; their colours become apparent when viewed through binoculars or a telescope.

Visibility

Apart from weather conditions, there are various factors that affect the visibility of stars on a given night. For many people the most significant is *light pollution*. At night, towns and cities abound with sources of artificial illumination: not only streetlights, but filling stations, shopfront illuminations, floodlights and security lights. Much of this light is directed upwards, drowning out starlight so that only the brightest stars remain visible. The urban stargazer must be prepared to search out an observing site as far away as possible from such interference.

A natural constraint on star brightness is atmospheric absorption. The lower the altitude of a star, the greater the amount of the Earth's atmosphere its light has to pass through before reaching the observer. Gas molecules in the atmosphere scatter starlight, deflecting some of it away from the observer, which makes stars closer to the horizon appear dimmer. The best time to view a star is therefore when it is highest in the sky. A further factor is eyesight: under ideal conditions, some-one with normal vision can see stars of magnitude 6.0, or a little fainter. Some people with extremely good eyesight have claimed to reach magnitude 7.0, and under exceptional conditions even 7.5.

However good your eyesight is, you need to allow some time under the night sky for your eyes to become adjusted to the low light levels. The human eye has two optical systems: day vision and night vision. When you step out into the dark from a brightly lit room, the night vision system takes time to build up to full strength. This process is called *dark adaptation* and for most people takes about 20 to 30 minutes. Subsequent ex-posure to artificial lights will put you back to square one. If you need to use a torch, use one that shines with a red light as this will not affect your dark adaptation.

The Milky Way

Anyone fortunate enough not to suffer from much light pollution will see, on a clear moonless night, a faint, hazy band of light arching right across the sky. This is the Milky Way – the concentrated light of the vast number of stars that lie between us and the rim of the Galaxy, the huge star system in which the Sun is located. The Galaxy has the overall form of a disk. From our vantage point within it, we see a greater concentration of stars close to the disk's plane than in other directions.

There is a greater concentration of bright stars in and near the Milky Way, which passes through some of the most prominent constellations: Aquila, Cygnus, Cassiopeia and Perseus in the northern hemisphere, passing close to Orion on the celestial equator, and Vela, Carina, Crux, Centaurus, Scorpius and Sagittarius in the southern hemisphere. The Milky Way is shown on the main charts (pages 13–18), but is omitted from the monthly charts.

Ecliptic and Zodiac

The ecliptic is the name given to the path that the Sun appears to follow over the course of the year. (It gets its name from the fact that the Moon has to be on the ecliptic for there to be an eclipse.) Stars along the ecliptic are of course invisible during the daytime, drowned out by the Sun's intense glare. The constellations containing these stars make up the zodiac.

The ecliptic, which is shown on the main charts, is in reality the projection on to the sky of the plane of the Earth's orbit around the Sun. Since most of the other planets of the Solar System orbit the Sun close to this plane, they appear in the sky close to the ecliptic. A bright 'star' near the ecliptic which is not on the charts is most likely a planet (see page 22).

Mapping the Stars

For the purposes of mapping, the most convenient way to conceive of the night sky is as a vast hollow sphere with the Earth at its centre. From wherever we stand on the surface of the Earth, one half of this sphere is visible at any one time, while the other half is invisible. This imaginary sphere is known as the *celestial sphere*. All the stars, though they are at different distances from the Earth, may then be depicted as if they occupied fixed positions on this sphere. (We imagine that the celestial sphere, with the stars fixed upon it, rotates once a day around the Earth, though we know that this isn't so.) Celestial cartographers are then faced with the same problem that confronts terrestrial map-makers: how to represent the curved surface of a sphere on a flat chart. The only essential difference is that terrestrial maps are drawn as if viewed from the outside, whereas celestial charts such as the ones in this book are prepared from an interior vantage point, looking out. The solution is much the same: find a projection that minimizes distortion of constellation shapes. The projections used for the charts in this book are described below.

Coordinates

Like terrestrial maps, celestial charts need to have a reference grid – a system of coordinates – laid upon them so that the positions of objects can be defined unambiguously. On terrestrial maps the coordinates are latitude and longitude. Latitude is measured from 0° to 90° north or south of the equator, while longitude is measured from 0° to 180° east or west of the Greenwich meridian. The celestial equivalents are similar. In place of latitude is *declination*, abbreviated 'dec'. Declination is measured from 0° at the *celestial equator* – the projection on to the celestial sphere of the Earth's equator – up or down to 90° at the celestial poles. A declination value preceded by a minus sign indicates a position in the southern hemisphere: −49°, for example, is below the celestial equator. If there is no sign (or a 'plus' sign) the declination is northerly: 49° (or +49°) is above the celestial equator.

The equivalent of longitude is called *right ascension*, abbreviated 'RA'. Right ascension is traditionally measured not in degrees, but in hours and minutes: from 0 to 24 hours, clockwise around the celestial equator. The starting point, corresponding to an RA of 0 hours – the celestial counterpart of the Greenwich meridian – is chosen to coincide with what is called the vernal equinox. This is the position on the celestial sphere where the Sun, in its annual journey along the ecliptic, crosses the celestial equator travelling from south to north. The vernal equinox lies in the constellation Pisces.

The position of a star or of any other celestial object is thus expressed as, for example, 'RA 6h 45m, dec −17°'.

The Main Charts

The six main charts (pages 13–18) cover the whole of the sky, with some overlap between them. Two show the regions round the north and south celestial poles (Charts 1 and 6), and four show a broad strip of the sky either side of the celestial equator (Charts 2 to 5). They fit together rather like the parts of a food can: Charts 1 and 6 are the top and bottom of the can, and Charts 2 to 5 between them form the cylindrical side. From the latitude of London, the stars on Chart 1 are visible throughout the year. But the stars on Charts 2 to 5, closer to the celestial equator, are not. Sometimes they are in the daytime sky, and on other occasions they may be visible only shortly after sunset or just before dawn. The seasons and dates when the stars on these charts are highest in the sky at 10 p.m. are at the top of each one. These dates tie in with the monthly charts.

Unavoidably, the projections used do introduce some distortion. This is more of a problem with Charts 2 to 5, which show stars to declinations of 60° north and south of the celestial equator. To depict the constellations in their correct shapes, the declination scale has been stretched at the top and bottom. This has the effect of making constellations on those parts of the charts look rather larger in relation to constellations near the celestial equator, compared with how they appear in the sky.

All 88 constellations are shown on these charts. The constellation names are all in capital letters, while star names are lower case with an initial capital. A few other features, for example prominent asterisms such as the Square of Pegasus, are in italic. The Milky Way is shown in a lighter blue than the main background. The ecliptic (the Sun's path against the background stars) is shown as a dashed red line. The Moon and the planets will always be found near the ecliptic. Over a thousand stars down to about magnitude 5.0 are shown. Each of the six charts has a magnitude scale. The brightest stars are shown in their true colours.

The Monthly Charts

Each pair of monthly charts between them show the whole of the night sky visible from the latitude of London at particular times and dates. These charts are also usable at latitudes further north or south. The only real difference will be with stars near the horizon, which

are, in any case, not easy to observe. The difference between chart and sky will become noticeable once you are 15° further north or south. They will serve their purpose very well for observing between the latitudes of 40°N and 60°N.

The main purpose of these charts is to help identify the constellations on view. Only the brightest stars are shown, roughly 200 on each pair of charts, down to third magnitude, with some fourth-magnitude stars to complete distinctive patterns. There is a little distortion resulting from the projection of the dome of the celestial sphere on to the flat page. This has the effect of making constellations near the horizon appear a little stretched.

First, use the calendar index (page 12) to find which pair of charts you need to use. Then locate the north pole star – Polaris – by using the stars of the Plough, as shown on Chart 1 (page 13). When you are looking at Polaris you are facing north, with west on your left and east on your right. (West and east are reversed on star charts because they show the view looking up into the sky instead of down towards the ground.) The left-hand chart then shows the view you have to the north. Most of the stars you see will be circumpolar, visible throughout the year.

Now turn and face the opposite direction, south. This is the view that changes most during the course of the year. Leo, with its prominent 'Sickle' asterism – a backward question-mark with bright Regulus as the dot – is high in the spring skies. Summer is dominated by the bright trio of Vega, Deneb and Altair overhead. Autumn's familiar marker is the Square of Pegasus, while the winter sky is ruled over by the stars of Orion.

Calendar Index to the Monthly Charts

To see which pair of monthly charts are appropriate for a particular time and date, find the time at the head of the diagram and follow the vertical column downwards to a point opposite the required date. The diagonal band in which this point lies shows the charts to be consulted. Remember to subtract one hour from your clock time if daylight saving time is in operation.

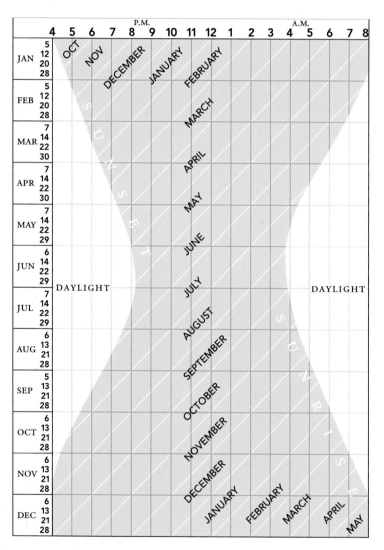

Chart 1: Northern Circumpolar Stars

This chart extends out to 51½° from the north celestial pole. It thus shows stars which are circumpolar as viewed from the latitude of London – in other words, from this latitude, these stars are above the horizon throughout the year.

The dates round the outside indicate when the lines of right ascension, making up the radial spokes of the coordinate grid, are aligned with the north point of the horizon at 10 p.m. For instance, on 22 April the 0h line of right ascension is to the north. Cassiopeia is quite low in the north, while on the other side of Polaris the stars of the Plough are

high in the sky. Polaris, marking the north celestial pole, is easily located from the stars at the end of the Plough, as indicated. These dates tie in with the positions of the stars as shown on the monthly charts.

The arrows indicate the apparent motion of the stars. Two hours of right ascension correspond to two hours of time. So, for example, by 12 p.m. on 22 April the sky will have rotated to bring the northern-most stars of Andromeda to just above the north point of horizon, and the 'bottom' of the chart will now be the point marked 2h/22 May.

Chart 2: Summer/Autumn

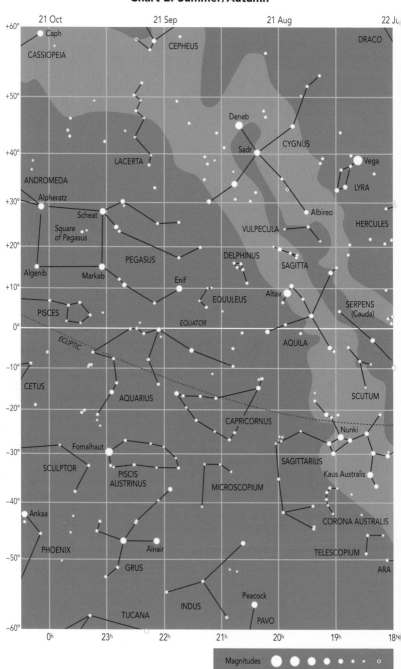

Magnitudes
-1 0 1 2 3 4 5 var.

Chart 3: Spring/Summer

Chart 4: Winter/Spring

Chart 5: Autumn/Winter

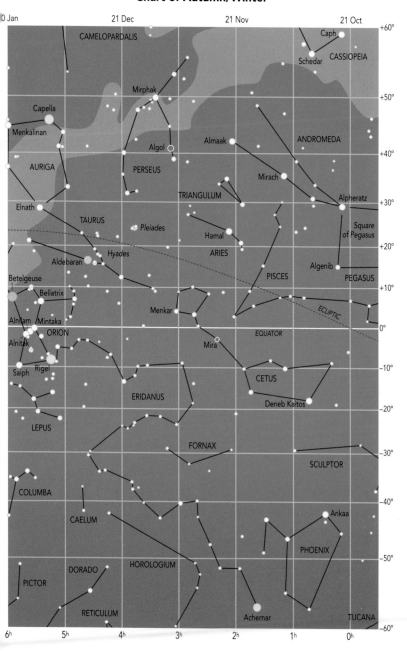

Chart 6: Southern Circumpolar Stars

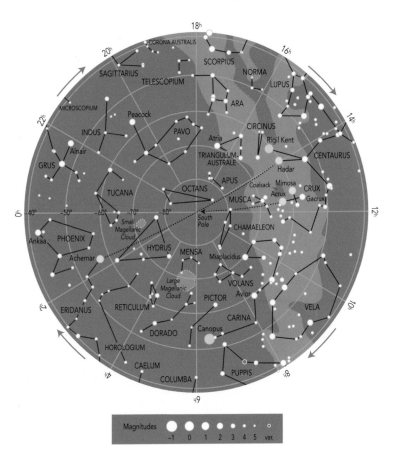

This chart extends out to 51½° from the south celestial pole, to a declination of 38½°. It thus shows stars which are permanently out of view from the latitude of London – in other words, from this latitude, these stars are below the horizon throughout the year.

Unlike its northern equivalent, the south celestial pole is not marked by a prominent star. Shown on the chart are two ways of locating it. The stars of the constellation Crux, the Cross, point towards the pole, which is also almost halfway between the bright stars Achernar, in Eridanus, and Hadar, in Centaurus.

The Constellations

The constellations and their names are approved by the International Astronomical Union.

Constellation	English name	Chart
Andromeda	Andromeda	1, 2, 5
Antlia	Air Pump	4
Apus	Bird of Paradise	6
Aquarius	Water Carrier	2
Aquila	Eagle	2
Ara	Altar	2, 3, 6
Aries	Ram	5
Auriga	Charioteer	1, 4, 5
Boötes	Herdsman	1, 3
Caelum	Chisel	5, 6
Camelopardalis	Giraffe	1, 5
Cancer	Crab	4
Canes Venatici	Hunting Dogs	1, 3
Canis Major	Great Dog	4
Canis Minor	Little Dog	4
Capricornus	Sea-Goat	2
Carina	Keel	4, 6
Cassiopeia	Cassiopeia	1, 2, 5
Centaurus	Centaur	3, 4, 6
Cepheus	Cepheus	1, 2
Cetus	Whale	2, 5
Chamaeleon	Chameleon	6
Circinus	Compasses	3, 6
Columba	Dove	4, 5, 6
Coma Berenices	Berenice's Hair	3, 4
Corona Australis	Southern Crown	2
Corona Borealis	Northern Crown	3
Corvus	Crow	3, 4
Crater	Cup	3, 4
Crux	Cross	3, 4, 6
Cygnus	Swan	1, 2
Delphinus	Dolphin	2
Dorado	Swordfish	5, 6
Draco	Dragon	1, 2, 3
Equuleus	Foal	2
Eridanus	River Eridanus	5, 6
Fornax	Furnace	5
Gemini	Twins	4
Grus	Crane	2
Hercules	Hercules	1, 2, 3
Horologium	Clock	5, 6
Hydra	Water Snake	3, 4
Hydrus	Little Water Snake	6
Indus	Indian	2
Lacerta	Lizard	1
Leo	Lion	3, 4
Leo Minor	Little Lion	4
Lepus	Hare	5
Libra	Scales	3
Lupus	Wolf	3, 6
Lynx	Lynx	1, 4
Lyra	Lyre	1, 2
Mensa	Table Mountain	6
Microscopium	Microscope	2
Monoceros	Unicorn	4
Musca	Fly	6
Norma	Square	3, 6
Octans	Octant	6
Ophiuchus	Serpent Bearer	3
Orion	Orion	4, 5
Pavo	Peacock	2, 6
Pegasus	Winged Horse	2, 5
Perseus	Perseus	1, 5
Phoenix	Phoenix	2, 5
Pictor	Painter's Easel	4, 5, 6
Pisces	Fishes	2, 5
Piscis Austrinus	Southern Fish	2
Puppis	Poop	4, 6
Pyxis	Ship's Compass	4
Reticulum	Net	5, 6
Sagitta	Arrow	2
Sagittarius	Archer	2, 3
Scorpius	Scorpion	3, 6
Sculptor	Sculptor	2, 5
Scutum	Shield	2
Serpens	Serpent	2, 3
Sextans	Sextant	4
Taurus	Bull	5
Telescopium	Telescope	2
Triangulum	Triangle	5
Triangulum Australe	Southern Triangle	6
Tucana	Toucan	2, 5
Ursa Major	Great Bear	1, 3, 4
Ursa Minor	Little Bear	1
Vela	Sails	4, 6
Virgo	Virgin	3, 4
Volans	Flying Fish	6
Vulpecula	Fox	2

Star Names

Listed here are all the stars named on the charts. They include all the brightest stars. Unlike constellation names, star names have no official status. There are many spelling variants: Almaak, for example, is sometimes spelt Almach or Alamak. Variant names also exist: Hadar, for example, is also known as Agena.

Star	Chart	Position RA	dec	Magnitude	Constellation
Achernar	5, 6	1h 38m	$-57°$	0.5	Eridanus
Acrux	6	12h 27m	$-63°$	0.8	Crux
Adhara	4	6h 59m	$-29°$	1.5	Canis Major
Albireo	2	19h 31m	28°	2.9	Cygnus
Alcor	1, 3	13h 25m	55°	4.0	Ursa Major
Aldebaran	5	4h 36m	17°	0.9	Taurus
Alderamin	1	21h 19m	63°	2.4	Cepheus
Algenib	2, 5	0h 13m	15°	2.8	Pegasus
Algieba	4	10h 20m	20°	1.9	Leo
Algol	1, 5	3h 08m	41°	2.1	Perseus
Alhena	4	6h 38m	16°	1.9	Gemini
Alioth	1, 3	12h 54m	56°	1.8	Ursa Major
Alkaid	1, 3	13h 48m	49°	1.9	Ursa Major
Almaak	1, 5	2h 04m	42°	2.3	Andromeda
Alnair	2, 6	22h 08m	$-47°$	1.7	Grus
Alnilam	5	5h 36m	$-1°$	1.7	Orion
Alnitak	5	5h 41m	$-2°$	1.9	Orion
Alphard	4	9h 28m	$-9°$	2.0	Hydra
Alphekka	3	15h 35m	27°	2.2	Corona Borealis
Alpheratz	2, 5	0h 08m	29°	2.1	Andromeda/Pegasus
Altair	2	19h 51m	9°	0.8	Aquila
Aludra	4	7h 24m	$-29°$	2.5	Canis Major
Ankaa	2, 5, 6	0h 26m	$-42°$	2.4	Phoenix
Antares	3	16h 29m	$-26°$	0.9	Scorpius
Arcturus	3	14h 16m	19°	0.0	Boötes
Atria	6	16h 49m	$-69°$	1.9	Triangulum Australe
Avior	4, 6	8h 23m	$-60°$	1.9	Carina
Bellatrix	5	5h 25m	6°	1.6	Orion
Betelgeuse	5	5h 55m	7°	0.5	Orion
Canopus	4	6h 24m	$-53°$	-0.7	Carina
Capella	1, 5	5h 17m	46°	0.1	Auriga
Caph	1, 2, 5	0h 09m	59°	2.3	Cassiopeia
Castor	4	7h 35m	32°	1.8	Gemini
Deneb Kaitos	5	0h 44m	$-18°$	2.0	Cetus
Deneb	1, 2	20h 41m	45°	1.3	Cygnus
Denebola	3, 4	11h 49m	15°	2.1	Leo
Dubhe	1	11h 04m	62°	1.8	Ursa Major
Elnath	5	5h 26m	29°	1.7	Taurus
Eltanin	1, 3	17h 57m	51°	2.2	Draco
Enif	1	21h 44m	10°	2.4	Pegasus

Star	Chart	Position		Magnitude	Constellation
		RA	dec		
Fomalhaut	2	22h 58m	−30°	1.2	Piscis Austrinus
Gacrux	3, 4, 6	12h 31m	−57°	1.6	Crux
Graffias	3	16h 05m	−20°	2.6	Scorpius
Hadar	6	14h 04m	−60°	0.6	Centaurus
Hamal	5	2h 07m	23°	2.0	Aries
Izar	3	14h 45m	27°	2.4	Boötes
Kaus Australis	2	18h 24m	−34°	1.9	Sagittarius
Kochab	1	14h 51m	74°	2.1	Ursa Minor
Markab	2	23h 05m	15°	2.5	Pegasus
Megrez	1, 3, 4	12h 15m	57°	3.3	Ursa Major
Menkalinan	1, 4, 5	6h 00m	45°	1.9	Auriga
Menkar	5	3h 02m	4°	2.5	Cetus
Menkent	3	14h 07m	−36°	2.1	Centaurus
Merak	1, 4	11h 02m	56°	2.4	Ursa Major
Miaplacidus	6	9h 13m	−70°	1.7	Carina
Mimosa	3, 6	12h 48m	−60°	1.2	Crux
Mintaka	5	5h 32m	0°	2.2	Orion
Mira	5	2h 19m	−3°	2.0	Cetus
Mirach	5	1h 10m	36°	2.1	Andromeda
Mirphak	1, 5	3h 24m	50°	1.8	Perseus
Mirzam	4	6h 23m	−18°	2.0	Canis Major
Mizar	1, 3	13h 24m	55°	2.3	Ursa Major
Nunki	2	18h 55m	−26°	2.0	Sagittarius
Peacock	2, 6	20h 26m	−57°	1.9	Pavo
Phecda	1, 3, 4	11h 54m	54°	2.4	Ursa Major
Polaris	1	2h 31m	89°	2.0	Ursa Minor
Pollux	4	7h 45m	28°	1.1	Gemini
Procyon	4	7h 39m	5°	0.4	Canis Minor
Rasalgethi	3	17h 15m	14°	3.1	Hercules
Rasalhague	3	17h 35m	13°	2.1	Ophiuchus
Regulus	4	10h 08m	12°	1.4	Leo
Rigel	5	5h 15m	−8°	0.1	Orion
Rigil Kent	6	14h 40m	−61°	−0.3	Centaurus
Sabik	3	17h 10m	−16°	2.4	Ophiuchus
Sadr	1, 2	20h 22m	40°	2.2	Cygnus
Saiph	5	5h 48m	−10°	2.1	Orion
Scheat	2	23h 04m	28°	2.4	Pegasus
Schedar	1, 5	0h 41m	57°	2.2	Cassiopeia
Shaula	3	17h 34m	−37°	1.6	Scorpius
Sirius	4	6h 45m	−17°	−1.5	Canis Major
Spica	3	13h 25m	−11°	1.0	Virgo
Vega	1, 2	18h 37m	39°	0.0	Lyra
Vindemiatrix	3	13h 02m	11°	2.8	Virgo
Wezen	4	7h 08m	−26°	1.8	Canis Major

Positions are to the nearest minute of RA and degree of declination. Magnitudes are correct to one decimal place. The magnitudes of double stars are combined, and those of variable stars are for maximum brightness.

The Planets

Any bright 'star' which you see near the ecliptic but is not on the star charts is almost certainly a planet. The planets cannot be plotted on star charts because they are continually changing their positions in the sky as they move in their orbits around the Sun. Six of the planets are bright enough to be seen from the Earth with the naked eye. They are, in order of their orbits around the Sun, Mercury, Venus, Mars, Jupiter, Saturn and Uranus. Uranus is very faint, but the other five rival and sometimes even outshine the brightest stars – Venus can actually be seen in the daytime, if you know exactly where to look.*

Mercury and Venus orbit closer to the Sun than the Earth does, and so are never far from the Sun in the sky. Mercury, the innermost planet, is so close to the Sun that it is glimpsed only occasionally in the twilight shortly after sunset or shortly before sunrise. Venus, though, may be visible as a brilliant beacon for over two hours after the Sun sets, when it is known as the evening star, or before the Sun rises, when it is called the morning star. Venus at its brightest has a magnitude of −4.7, 20 times as bright as Sirius, the brightest star. Mercury can reach magnitude −1.7, but never seems particularly bright as it is always viewed near the horizon in a twilit sky.

Both these planets orbit the Sun quite quickly, and their positions in the sky are seen to change over the course of a few nights. But Mars, Jupiter and Saturn have orbits outside the Earth's and consequently move more slowly. They take, respectively, nearly two years, nearly 12 years, and 29½ years to orbit the Sun. Although the change in position of Mars soon becomes noticeable, Jupiter and, in particular, Saturn will need to be observed for several weeks before their motion against the stars of the zodiacal constellations is apparent.

After Venus, Jupiter is the brightest of the planets, reaching magnitude −2.9 when its orbit brings it nearest the Earth. Saturn at its brightest is magnitude −0.8.

These two are giant planets, around ten times the Earth's diameter. But Mars is small – half the size of the Earth – and its distance from Earth varies widely over the course of its orbit. Its brightness therefore also varies widely, but at maximum it rivals Jupiter, at magnitude −2.8.

The tables on the opposite page show where to locate Venus, Mars, Jupiter and Saturn on the main charts for each month of the year up to December 2014. (As Mercury orbits the Sun in only 88 days, its movements cannot be plotted at monthly intervals.) The tables give the planet's right ascension (RA), in hours and minutes, for the first day of each month. Look up the RA for the date nearest the one you require, and find this RA value along the bottom edge of Charts 2 to 5. (For the faster-moving Venus and Mars, it may help to estimate an intermediate RA for a position near the middle of a month.) The RA values are correct to the nearest 4 minutes. On the scale of Charts 2 to 5, this corresponds very nearly to 1 mm. Now imagine a line drawn vertically up the chart from the point you have located. The planet will be found close to the position where this line crosses the ecliptic. The tables can also be used in reverse, to identify a planet. Estimate its RA by locating nearby stars on the charts, then consult the tables to see which planet should be near that position.

* Don't look for Venus when it is near the Sun: you will risk permanent damage to your eyesight, and in any case the planet will be invisible in the Sun's glare. And *never* look at the Sun through binoculars or a telescope.

VENUS

Year	Jan	Feb	Mar	Apr	May	Jun	Jul	Aug	Sep	Oct	Nov	Dec
2005	17 12	20 00	22 20	00 44	03 04	05 44	08 24	10 52	13 04	15 16	17 40	19 36
2006	20 56	19 08	19 52	21 48	23 52	02 04	04 28	07 08	09 44	12 04	14 28	17 04
2007	19 52	22 28	00 36	02 56	05 24	07 52	09 40	10 12	09 12	09 44	11 32	13 36
2008	16 00	18 40	21 12	23 40	01 56	04 28	07 08	09 44	12 08	14 24	17 00	19 36
2009	22 00	23 52	00 44	00 04	00 08	01 36	03 36	06 00	08 36	11 00	13 20	15 48
2010	18 40	21 23	23 37	01 58	04 25	07 08	09 33	11 40	13 26	14 31	13 56	13 57
2011	15 32	17 49	20 07	22 35	00 51	03 14	05 48	08 31	11 02	13 19	15 49	18 30
2012	21 07	23 29	01 31	03 37	05 15	05 10	04 26	05 35	07 41	09 58	12 17	14 36
2013	17 15	20 03	22 23	00 46	03 07	05 48	08 26	10 53	13 06	15 17	17 40	19 34
2014	19 53	18 55	19 48	21 47	23 53	02 07	04 29	07 09	09 47	12 07	14 31	17 06

MARS

Year	Jan	Feb	Mar	Apr	May	Jun	Jul	Aug	Sep	Oct	Nov	Dec
2005	16 08	17 44	19 08	20 44	22 12	23 28	00 52	02 04	03 00	03 28	03 00	02 24
2006	02 32	03 16	04 12	05 28	06 44	08 04	09 16	10 32	11 44	12 56	14 12	15 36
2007	17 08	18 48	20 20	21 56	23 40	00 48	02 12	03 36	04 56	06 04	06 48	06 48
2008	06 00	05 32	05 56	06 48	07 52	09 00	10 08	11 20	12 32	13 36	15 08	16 36
2009	18 16	19 56	21 28	23 00	00 24	01 52	03 20	04 48	06 16	07 36	08 40	09 24
2010	09 29	08 49	08 16	08 24	09 04	10 00	11 00	12 07	13 19	14 36	16 05	17 40
2011	19 23	21 04	22 31	00 01	01 26	02 55	04 24	05 56	07 24	08 42	09 52	10 48
2012	11 28	11 39	11 10	10 31	10 31	11 05	11 55	12 58	14 11	15 32	17 07	18 46
2013	20 29	22 06	23 28	00 56	02 22	03 52	05 22	06 53	08 19	09 35	10 47	11 49
2014	12 45	13 29	13 46	13 24	12 44	12 36	13 06	14 01	15 14	16 39	18 17	19 56

JUPITER

Year	Jan	Feb	Mar	Apr	May	Jun	Jul	Aug	Sep	Oct	Nov	Dec
2005	13 04	13 12	13 08	12 56	12 40	12 36	12 40	12 52	13 08	13 32	13 56	14 24
2006	14 44	15 00	15 08	15 04	14 48	14 36	14 28	14 32	14 44	15 04	15 32	16 00
2007	16 28	16 52	17 08	17 16	17 12	16 56	16 44	16 32	16 36	16 52	17 16	17 44
2008	18 12	18 44	19 08	19 28	19 36	19 32	19 20	19 04	18 56	19 00	19 12	19 36
2009	20 04	20 36	21 00	21 28	21 44	21 56	21 56	21 48	21 32	21 20	21 24	21 36
2010	21 56	22 22	22 48	23 15	23 39	00 00	00 12	00 14	00 06	23 51	23 40	23 39
2011	23 50	00 09	00 31	00 58	01 25	01 51	02 12	02 28	02 33	02 27	02 12	01 59
2012	01 54	02 03	02 18	02 44	03 11	03 41	04 09	04 34	04 53	05 00	04 55	04 40
2013	04 24	04 17	04 23	04 41	05 05	05 34	06 04	06 34	07 00	07 19	07 28	07 24
2014	07 09	06 52	06 45	06 49	07 04	07 27	07 54	08 23	08 50	09 13	09 31	09 40

SATURN

Year	Jan	Feb	Mar	Apr	May	Jun	Jul	Aug	Sep	Oct	Nov	Dec
2005	07 48	07 36	07 28	07 28	07 36	07 44	08 00	08 16	08 32	08 44	08 52	08 52
2006	08 48	08 36	08 28	08 24	08 28	08 36	08 52	09 08	09 24	09 36	09 48	09 52
2007	09 48	09 40	09 32	09 24	09 24	09 32	09 40	09 56	10 08	10 24	10 36	10 40
2008	10 44	10 36	10 28	10 20	10 16	10 20	10 28	10 40	10 56	11 08	11 20	11 28
2009	11 32	11 32	11 24	11 16	11 08	11 08	11 12	11 24	11 36	11 52	12 04	12 16
2010	12 20	12 20	12 14	12 06	11 59	11 56	11 59	12 07	12 19	12 32	12 46	12 57
2011	03 05	03 07	03 04	12 56	12 48	12 43	12 43	12 49	13 00	13 12	13 26	13 39
2012	13 48	13 53	13 51	13 45	13 36	13 29	13 27	13 31	13 40	13 52	14 06	14 19
2013	14 31	14 38	14 39	14 34	14 25	14 17	14 13	14 14	14 21	14 32	14 46	15 00
2014	15 13	15 22	15 25	15 23	15 15	15 06	15 00	14 59	15 04	15 14	15 27	15 42

The Moon

When strong moonlight makes it difficult to observe the stars, turn your attention to the Moon itself. Some of its features are marked on this pair of photographs, showing the Moon at last quarter, a week after it is full (left), and at first quarter, a week before it is full (right). The largest of these features are apparent to the naked eye. Binoculars or a small telescope will show many more.

'Mare' means 'sea'. Astronomers once thought that the Moon was Earth-like, but

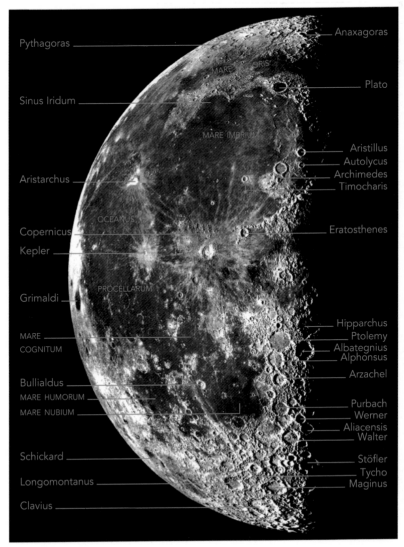

Pythagoras

Sinus Iridum

Aristarchus

Copernicus

Kepler

Grimaldi

MARE COGNITUM

Bullialdus

MARE HUMORUM

MARE NUBIUM

Schickard

Longomontanus

Clavius

MARE IMBRIUM

OCEANUS

PROCELLARUM

Anaxagoras

Plato

Aristillus

Autolycus

Archimedes

Timocharis

Eratosthenes

Hipparchus

Ptolemy

Albategnius

Alphonsus

Arzachel

Purbach

Werner

Aliacensis

Walter

Stöfler

Tycho

Maginus

these dark areas are in fact solidified lava which flooded into giant impact craters formed when the Moon was young. The maria have rather fanciful names: Oceanus Procellarum means 'Ocean of Storms', while Mare Serenitatis is the 'Sea of Serenity'. The craters are named mostly after famous astronomers of the past.

The visibility of lunar features depends on the Moon's phase. At full Moon, for example, the surface appears very bright and some features are hard to see.

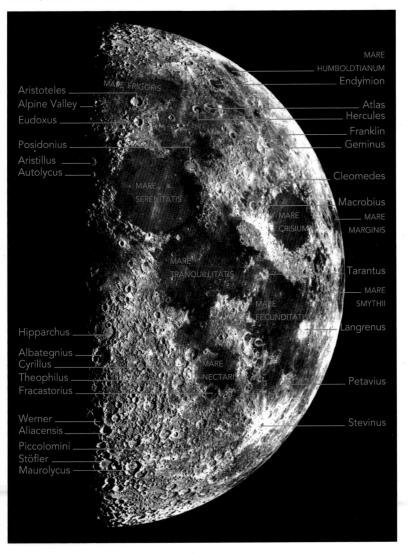

January – Looking North

The main constellations visible on January evenings. The positions are correct for 5 January at 11 p.m. and 20 January at 10 p.m. Use this pair of charts for other dates and times in January, for four minutes later each previous night, or four minutes earlier each following night: for example, 4 January at 11.04 p.m., 6 January at 10.56 p.m. or 10 January at 10.40 p.m.

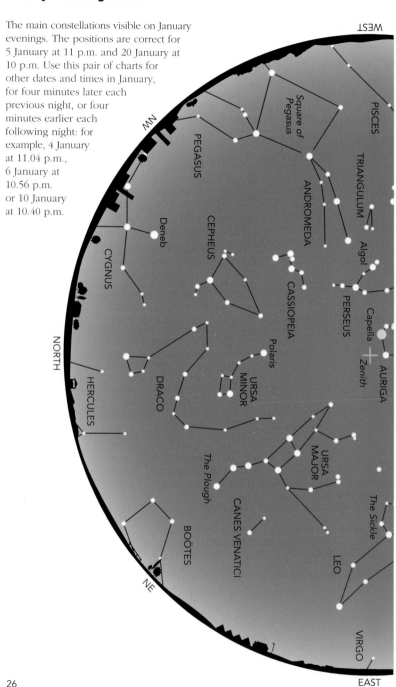

Times in other months for which the chart may be used are indicated in the calendar index (page 12). In two hours the celestial sphere rotates so that the stars will have moved from the positions shown here to those shown on the February charts.

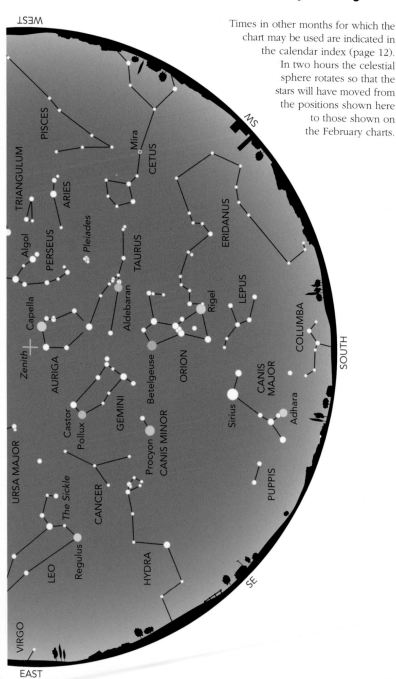

WEST

PISCES

TRIANGULUM

PERSEUS

ARIES

Algol

Pleiades

Mira

CETUS

TAURUS

Aldebaran

ERIDANUS

LEPUS

Rigel

COLUMBA

SW

SOUTH

Capella

Zenith

AURIGA

ORION

Betelgeuse

CANIS MAJOR

Adhara

Castor

Pollux

GEMINI

Sirius

Procyon

CANIS MINOR

PUPPIS

URSA MAJOR

The Sickle

CANCER

HYDRA

SE

LEO

Regulus

VIRGO

EAST

27

February – Looking North

The main constellations visible on February evenings. The positions are correct for 5 February at 11 p.m. and 20 February at 10 p.m. Use this pair of charts for other dates and times in February, for four minutes later each previous night, or four minutes earlier each following night: for example, 4 February at 11.04 p.m., 6 February at 10.56 p.m. or 10 February at 10.40 p.m.

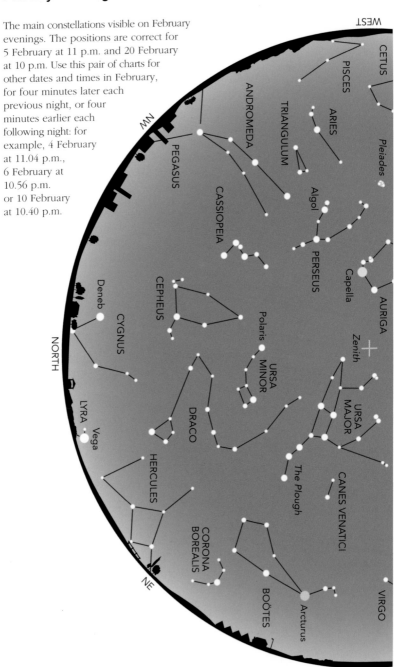

Times in other months for which the chart may be used are indicated in the calendar index (page 12). In two hours the celestial sphere rotates so that the stars will have moved from the positions shown here to those shown on the March charts.

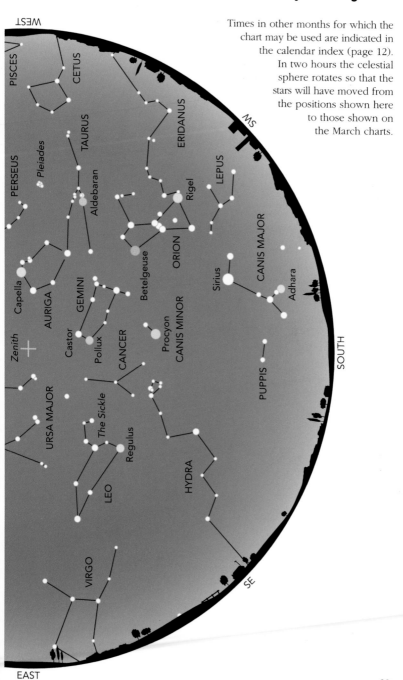

WEST

PISCES

CETUS

PERSEUS

TAURUS

Pleiades

Aldebaran

ERIDANUS

Rigel

LEPUS

SSW

AURIGA

Capella

GEMINI

Castor

Pollux

Betelgeuse

ORION

CANIS MAJOR

Sirius

Adhara

Zenith

CANCER

Procyon

CANIS MINOR

CANIS MAJOR

URSA MAJOR

The Sickle

Regulus

HYDRA

PUPPIS

SOUTH

LEO

VIRGO

SE

EAST

March – Looking North

The main constellations visible on March evenings. The positions are correct for 5 March at 11 p.m. and 20 March at 10 p.m. Use this pair of charts for other dates and times in March, for four minutes later each previous night, or four minutes earlier each following night: for example, 4 March at 11.04 p.m., 6 March at 10.56 p.m. or 10 March at 10.40 p.m.

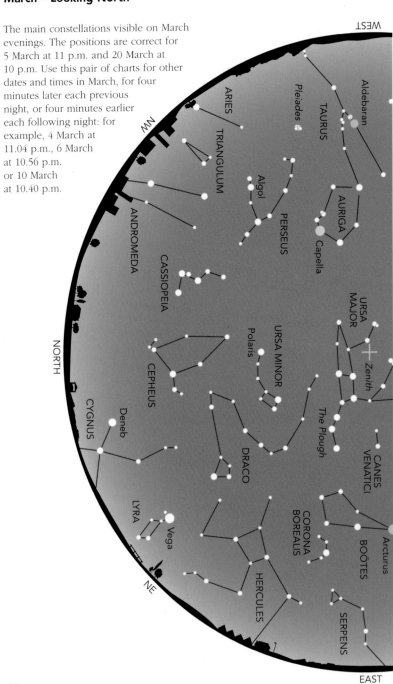

WEST

Aldebaran
Pleiades
ARIES
TAURUS
NW
TRIANGULUM
Algol
AURIGA
PERSEUS
Capella
ANDROMEDA
CASSIOPEIA
URSA MAJOR
Polaris
URSA MINOR
Zenith
NORTH
CEPHEUS
The Plough
CYGNUS
Deneb
DRACO
CANES VENATICI
LYRA
Vega
CORONA BOREALIS
Arcturus
BOÖTES
NE
HERCULES
SERPENS
EAST

Times in other months for which the chart may be used are indicated in the calendar index (page 12). In two hours the celestial sphere rotates so that the stars will have moved from the positions shown here to those shown on the April charts.

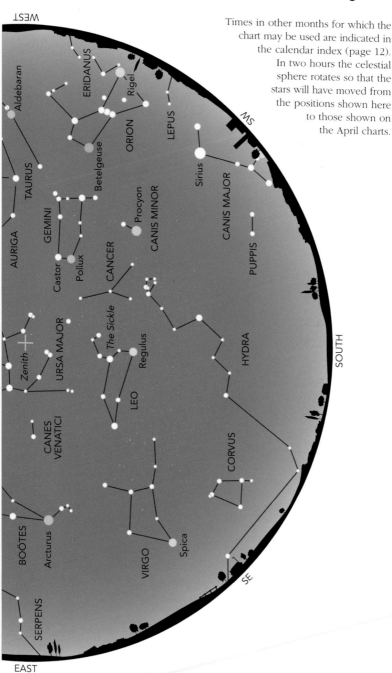

WEST

EAST

WEST

SOUTH

SE

SW

Aldebaran

ERIDANUS

Rigel

ORION

LEPUS

Betelgeuse

Sirius

CANIS MAJOR

TAURUS

AURIGA

GEMINI

Procyon

CANIS MINOR

PUPPIS

Castor

Pollux

CANCER

The Sickle

Zenith

URSA MAJOR

Regulus

HYDRA

LEO

CANES
VENATICI

CORVUS

BOÖTES

Arcturus

VIRGO

Spica

SERPENS

April – Looking North

The main constellations visible on April evenings. The positions are correct for 5 April at 11 p.m. and 20 April at 10 p.m. Use this pair of charts for other dates and times in April, for four minutes later each previous night, or four minutes earlier each following night: for example, 4 April at 11.04 p.m., 6 April at 10.56 p.m. or 10 April at 10.40 p.m.

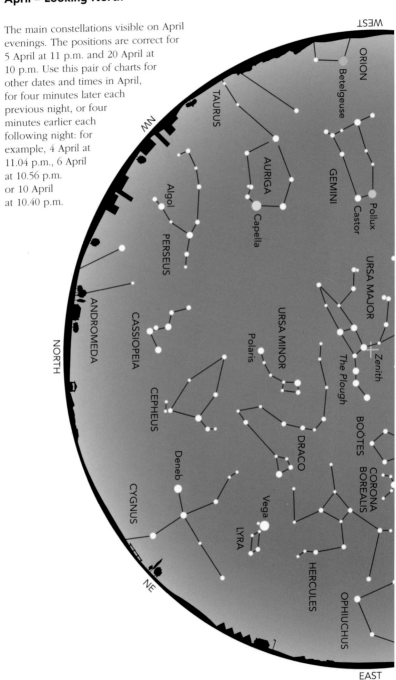

Times in other months for which the chart may be used are indicated in the calendar index (page 12). In two hours the celestial sphere rotates so that the stars will have moved from the positions shown here to those shown on the May charts.

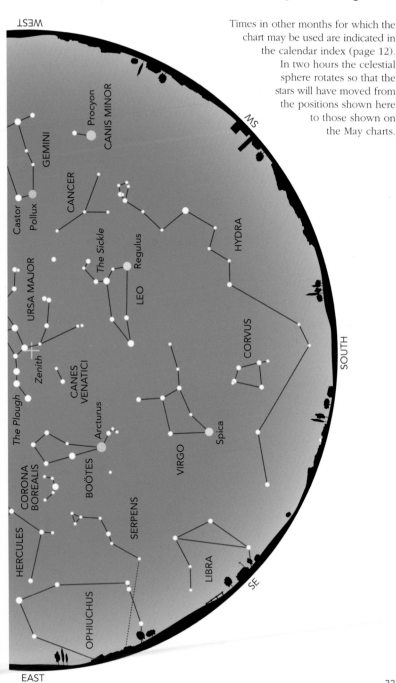

33

May – Looking North

The main constellations visible on May evenings. The positions are correct for 5 May at 11 p.m. and 20 May at 10 p.m. Use this pair of charts for other dates and times in May, for four minutes later each previous night, or four minutes earlier each following night: for example, 4 May at 11.04 p.m., 6 May at 10.56 p.m. or 10 May at 10.40 p.m.

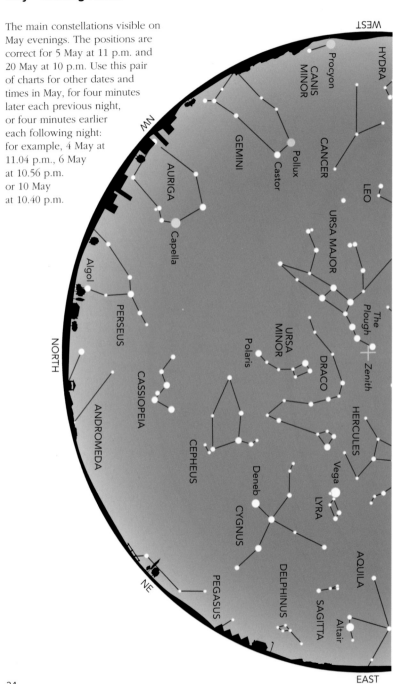

WEST

HYDRA

CANIS MINOR

Procyon

GEMINI

CANCER

Pollux

Castor

AURIGA

LEO

Capella

URSA MAJOR

Algol

The Plough

PERSEUS

Zenith

NORTH

Polaris

URSA MINOR

DRACO

HERCULES

CASSIOPEIA

ANDROMEDA

CEPHEUS

Vega

Deneb

LYRA

CYGNUS

PEGASUS

DELPHINUS

AQUILA

NE

SAGITTA

Altair

EAST

Times in other months for which the chart may be used are indicated in the calendar index (page 12). In two hours the celestial sphere rotates so that the stars will have moved from the positions shown here to those shown on the June charts.

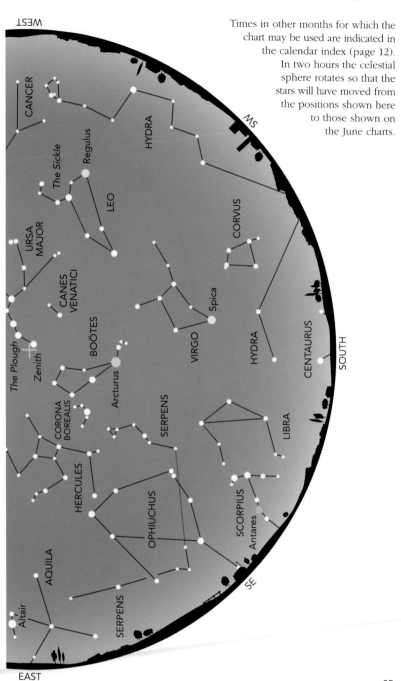

June – Looking North

The main constellations visible on June
evenings. The positions are correct for
5 June at 11 p.m. and 20 June at 10 p.m.
Use this pair of charts for other dates
and times in June, for four minutes
later each previous night,
or four minutes earlier
each following night:
for example, 4 June at
11.04 p.m., 6 June
at 10.56 p.m.
or 10 June
at 10.40 p.m.

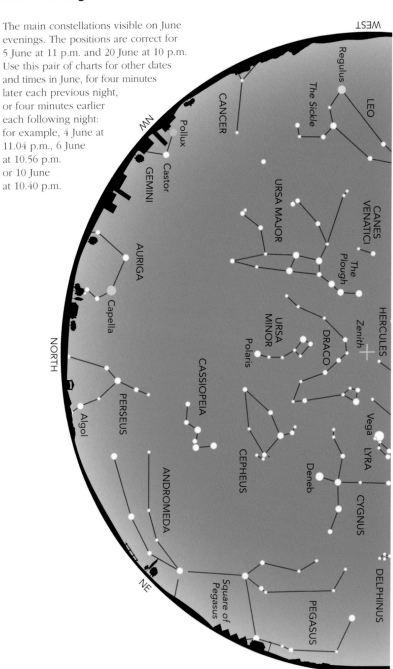

WEST

Regulus

LEO

The Sickle

CANCER

Pollux

NW

Castor

GEMINI

URSA MAJOR

CANES VENATICI

The Plough

AURIGA

Capella

HERCULES

Zenith

URSA MINOR

DRACO

Polaris

NORTH

CASSIOPEIA

PERSEUS

Algol

Vega

LYRA

CEPHEUS

ANDROMEDA

Deneb

CYGNUS

NE

Square of Pegasus

PEGASUS

DELPHINUS

EAST

Times in other months for which the chart may be used are indicated in the calendar index (page 12). In two hours the celestial sphere rotates so that the stars will have moved from the positions shown here to those shown on the July charts.

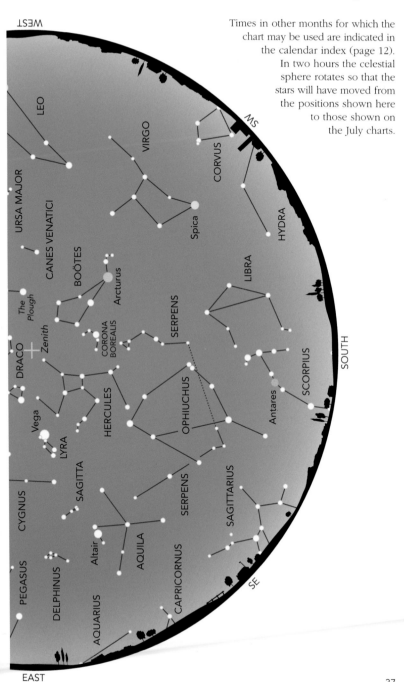

WEST

LEO

VIRGO

CORVUS

URSA MAJOR

CANES VENATICI

HYDRA

Spica

The Plough

BOÖTES

Arcturus

LIBRA

SERPENS

DRACO

Zenith

CORONA BOREALIS

SW

SOUTH

SCORPIUS

Vega

HERCULES

OPHIUCHUS

Antares

LYRA

CYGNUS

SAGITTA

SERPENS

SAGITTARIUS

PEGASUS

DELPHINUS

Altair

AQUILA

CAPRICORNUS

SE

AQUARIUS

EAST

37

July – Looking North

The main constellations visible on July evenings. The positions are correct for 5 July at 11 p.m. and 20 July at 10 p.m. Use this pair of charts for other dates and times in July, for four minutes later each previous night, or four minutes earlier each following night: for example, 4 July at 11.04 p.m., 6 July at 10.56 p.m. or 10 July at 10.40 p.m.

Times in other months for which the chart may be used are indicated in the calendar index (page 12). In two hours the celestial sphere rotates so that the stars will have moved from the positions shown here to those shown on the August charts.

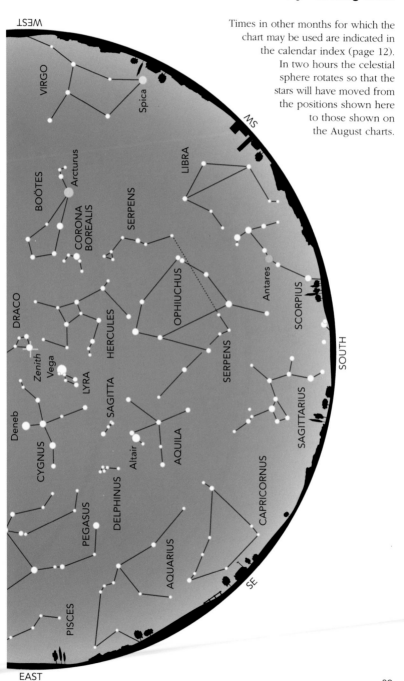

WEST

VIRGO

Spica

SW

LIBRA

Arcturus

BOÖTES

SERPENS

CORONA BOREALIS

OPHIUCHUS

Antares

SCORPIUS

DRACO

HERCULES

SERPENS

Zenith
Vega

LYRA

SAGITTA

SAGITTARIUS

SOUTH

Deneb

CYGNUS

Altair

AQUILA

CAPRICORNUS

PEGASUS

DELPHINUS

AQUARIUS

SE

PISCES

EAST

August – Looking North

The main constellations visible on August
evenings. The positions are correct for
5 August at 11 p.m. and 20 August at
10 p.m. Use this pair of charts for other
dates and times in August, for
four minutes later each previous
night, or four minutes earlier
each following night: for
example, 4 August at
11.04 p.m., 6 August
at 10.56 p.m.
or 10 August
at 10.40 p.m.

Times in other months for which the chart may be used are indicated in the calendar index (page 12). In two hours the celestial sphere rotates so that the stars will have moved from the positions shown here to those shown on the September charts.

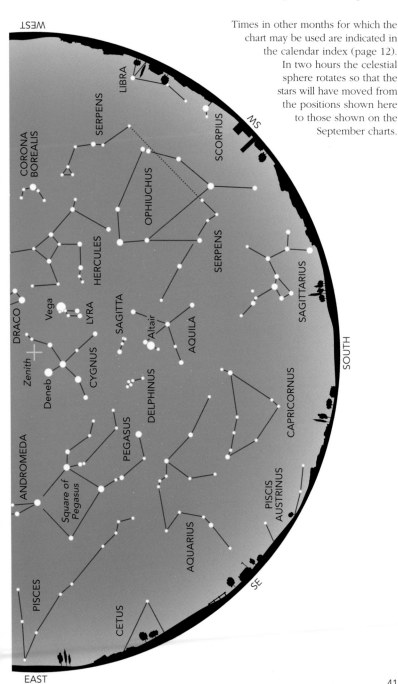

September – Looking North

The main constellations visible on September evenings. The positions are correct for 5 September at 11 p.m. and 20 September at 10 p.m. Use this pair of charts for other dates and times in September, for four minutes later each previous night, or four minutes earlier each following night: for example, 4 September at 11.04 p.m., 6 September at 10.56 p.m. or 10 September at 10.40 p.m.

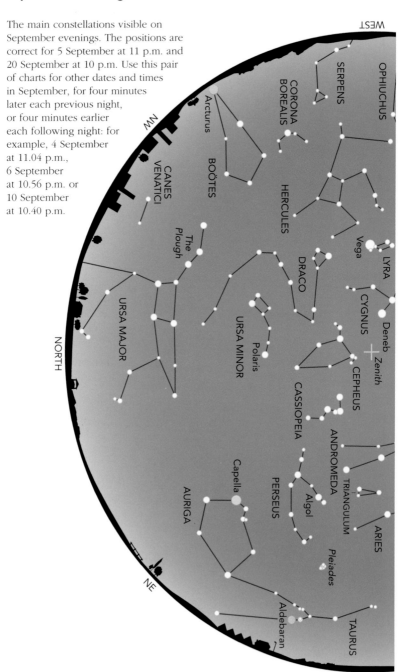

WEST

NW

NORTH

NE

EAST

OPHIUCHUS
SERPENS
CORONA BOREALIS
Arcturus
BOÖTES
CANES VENATICI
HERCULES
The Plough
DRACO
Vega
LYRA
CYGNUS
Deneb
Zenith
URSA MAJOR
URSA MINOR
Polaris
CEPHEUS
CASSIOPEIA
ANDROMEDA
TRIANGULUM
ARIES
Capella
PERSEUS
Algol
AURIGA
Pleiades
Aldebaran
TAURUS

Times in other months for which the chart may be used are indicated in the calendar index (page 12). In two hours the celestial sphere rotates so that the stars will have moved from the positions shown here to those shown on the October charts.

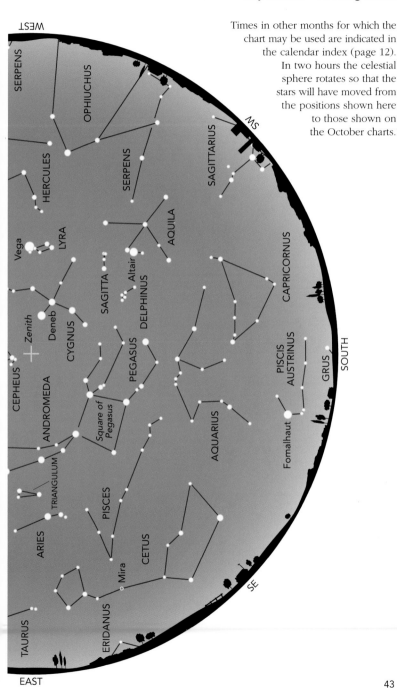

October – Looking North

The main constellations visible on
October evenings. The positions are
correct for 5 October at 11 p.m. and
20 October at 10 p.m. Use this pair
of charts for other dates and times
in October, for four minutes
later each previous night,
or four minutes earlier
each following night:
for example, 4 October
at 11.04 p.m.,
6 October at
10.56 p.m. or
10 October
at 10.40 p.m.

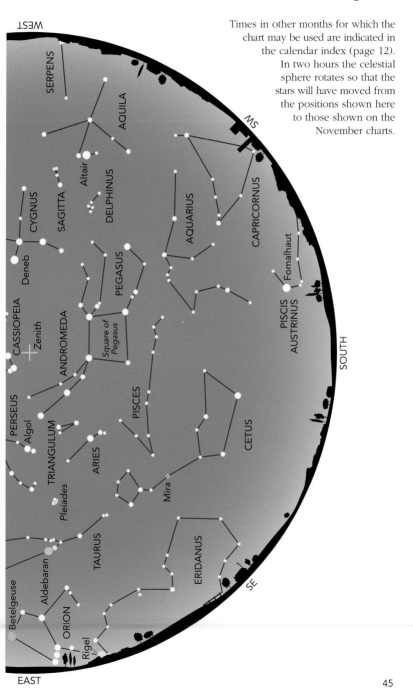

Times in other months for which the chart may be used are indicated in the calendar index (page 12). In two hours the celestial sphere rotates so that the stars will have moved from the positions shown here to those shown on the November charts.

WEST

SERPENS

AQUILA

Altair

CYGNUS

SAGITTA

DELPHINUS

Deneb

AQUARIUS

CAPRICORNUS

Fomalhaut

PEGASUS

CASSIOPEIA

Zenith

ANDROMEDA

Square of Pegasus

PISCIS AUSTRINUS

SOUTH

PERSEUS

Algol

PISCES

CETUS

TRIANGULUM

ARIES

Pleiades

Mira

TAURUS

ERIDANUS

Betelgeuse

Aldebaran

ORION

Rigel

EAST

45

November – Looking North

The main constellations visible on November evenings. The positions are correct for 5 November at 11 p.m. and 20 November at 10 p.m. Use this pair of charts for other dates and times in November, for four minutes later each previous night, or four minutes earlier each following night: for example, 4 November at 11.04 p.m., 6 November at 10.56 p.m. or 10 November at 10.40 p.m.

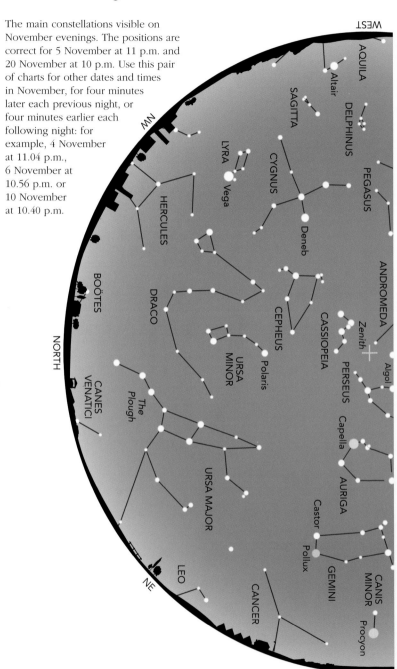

Times in other months for which the chart may be used are indicated in the calendar index (page 12). In two hours the celestial sphere rotates so that the stars will have moved from the positions shown here to those shown on the December charts.

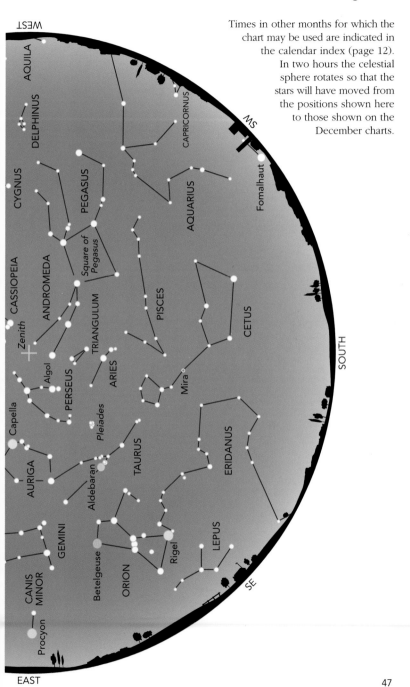

47

December – Looking North

The main constellations visible on December evenings. The positions are correct for 5 December at 11 p.m. and 20 December at 10 p.m. Use this pair of charts for other dates and times in December, for four minutes later each previous night, or four minutes earlier each following night: for example, 4 December at 11.04 p.m., 6 December at 10.56 p.m. or 10 December at 10.40 p.m.

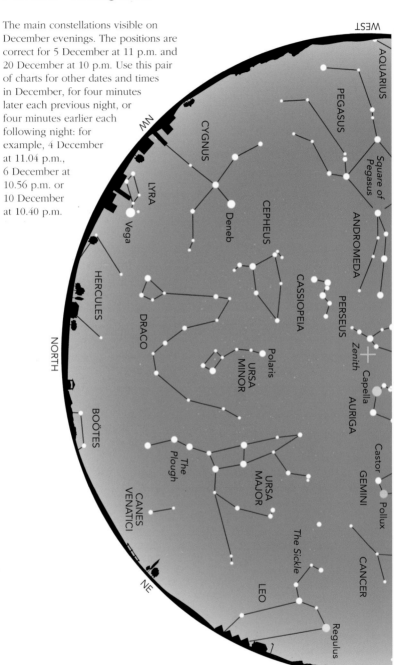

Times in other months for which the chart may be used are indicated in the calendar index (page 12). In two hours the celestial sphere rotates so that the stars will have moved from the positions shown here to those shown on the January charts.

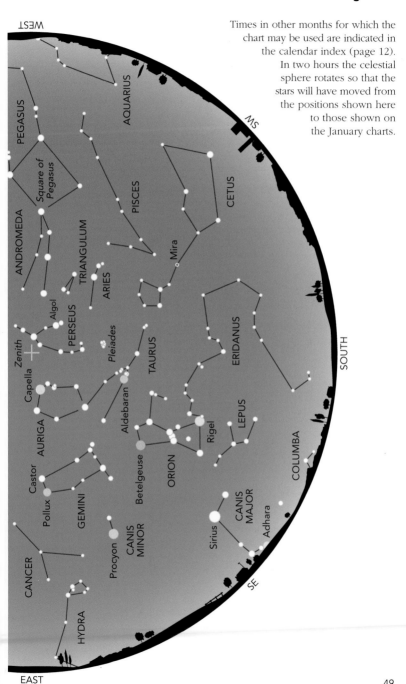

WEST

SM

SOUTH

PEGASUS

AQUARIUS

Square of Pegasus

PISCES

CETUS

ANDROMEDA

TRIANGULUM

ARIES

Mira

Algol

PERSEUS

TAURUS

Zenith

Pleiades

ERIDANUS

Capella

Aldebaran

AURIGA

LEPUS

Rigel

Castor

Betelgeuse

ORION

COLUMBA

GEMINI

Pollux

CANIS MAJOR

Procyon

CANIS MINOR

Sirius

Adhara

CANCER

SE

HYDRA

EAST

Constellations as Pointers

Some of the most prominent groups of stars are also the best celestial signposts.

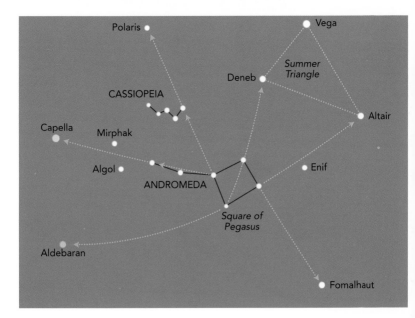

Make full use of these pointers when you start finding your way about the night sky.

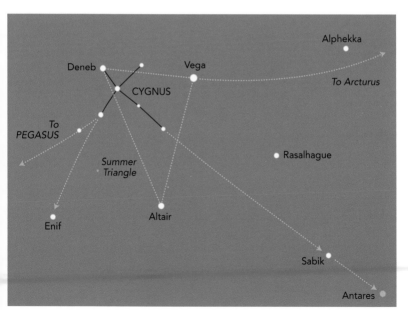

Finder Charts

These four pages show larger-scale charts which will help you to locate some of the best examples of different types of celestial object: a double star, two variable stars, two star clusters, a nebula and a galaxy. All of them can be seen with the naked eye, though binoculars or a small telescope will of course give better views.

Albireo, a double star

Many stars in the sky are *double stars*: binoculars or a telescope show not one star but a pair. Some double stars make fine targets for owners of small telescopes, because they show interesting colour contrasts. One of the most beautiful is Albireo (below), in the constellation Cygnus (Chart 2), which consists of a third-magnitude orange star with a fifth-magnitude blue companion. The pair can be separated with high-power binoculars or a small telescope. Another famous pair, for which you need only your unaided eye, are the stars Mizar and Alcor in the Plough (Chart 1). A small telescope will show that Mizar itself is a double star.

Two variable stars: Delta Cephei and Mira

While most stars shine with a constant luminosity, others – called *variable stars* – fluctuate in their light output, usually because they are pulsating. A famous example is the star Delta Cephei, in the constellation Cepheus (Chart 1), which varies between magnitudes 3.5 and 4.4 in a regular period of 5.37 days. Another famous pulsating star is Mira, in Cetus (Chart 5), but this is an irregular variable. Its period is roughly 330 days, and it can be as bright as magnitude 2.0, or as faint as 10.1 – well below naked-eye visibility. The charts on the right show the magnitudes of nearby stars for comparison. Try to estimate the brightness of these two stars on different occasions.

Finder Charts

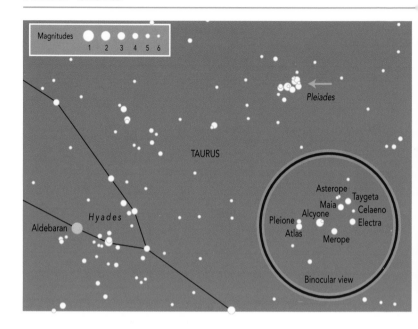

Star clusters: Pleiades and Hyades

Some stars reside not alone or in pairs, but in *star clusters*, groups that may have anywhere from a dozen to a million members. Most striking to the naked eye are two clusters in the constellation Taurus (Chart 5). The Pleiades are also known as the Seven Sisters, seven being the number many people can see. The cluster looks something like a miniature version of the Plough. To the east of the Pleiades are the Hyades, a much less compact grouping of stars whose brightest members form a V shape near the bright orange star Aldebaran (which is not a member of the cluster).

The Orion Nebula

As well as stars, our Galaxy contains *nebulae*, huge clouds of gas and dust – the raw materials from which stars are made. In some nebulae stars are actually in the process of being born. This is happening in the Orion Nebula (top right), in the constellation Orion (Chart 5), situated just below Orion's Belt. The light of the new stars is illuminating the nebula, making it visible to the naked eye as a faint misty patch. The Coalsack in Crux (Chart 6) is another nebula, but no stars illuminate its gas, so it appears dark.

The Andromeda Galaxy

Our own Galaxy, which we see on a clear night as the Milky Way, is but one of countless millions in the universe. Only a handful are visible to the naked eye. Two dwarf galaxies, companions of our own, are the Magellanic Clouds (Chart 6). The only other large galaxy visible to the naked eye is the Andromeda Galaxy (bottom right), in the constellation Andromeda (Chart 5), seen as an elongated blur on a clear night.

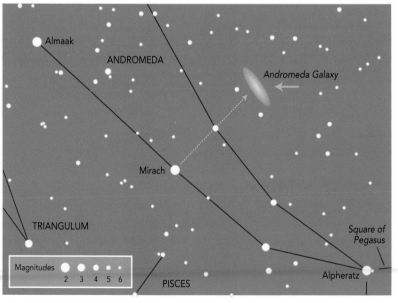

Notes on the Constellations

The name of each constellation is followed by the number of the main chart(s) on which it is shown, together with its approximate position in right ascension (RA) and declination (dec), and the first monthly chart on which it appears (if no month is given, the constellation is either faint or in the far south). All the constellations are listed here, even the small ones that contain nothing of interest to the naked-eye observer. The most favourable times of year mentioned are when the particular constellation is highest in the sky in the late evening.

ANDROMEDA
Charts 1, 2, 5; RA 1h dec 40°; January
Andromeda is on the opposite side of Cassiopeia from Polaris. Its brightest stars, including the second-magnitude Mirach and Almaak, stretch away from the north-east corner of the Square of Pegasus. Alpheratz (also known as Sirrah), the star marking that corner, officially belongs to Andromeda rather than Pegasus. This constellation is most conspicuous in the autumn and early winter, but is visible nearly all the year round. Discernible as a fuzzy patch to the naked eye in a clear sky is the Andromeda Galaxy (pages 54–55). This is the closest large galaxy beyond the Milky Way, and is the most distant object visible without a telescope or binoculars.

ANTLIA
Chart 4; RA 10h dec −30°

APUS
Chart 6; RA 15h dec −80°

AQUARIUS
Chart 2; RA 22h dec −10°; June
Aquarius lies between the Square of Pegasus and the bright star Fomalhaut, in Piscis Austrinus. This constellation, one of the 12 making up the zodiac, is one of the largest but contains no stars brighter than third magnitude. Aquarius is best placed for observation in the late autumn and early winter.

AQUILA
Chart 2; RA 20h dec 0°; May
Aquila lies in a rich part of the Milky Way, just north of the celestial equator. Its brightest star, the first-magnitude Altair, shines with a white radiance. Altair and the two fainter stars either side of it make a line which points towards Vega (in Lyra). Together with Deneb (in Cygnus), Vega and Altair form what has become known as the Summer Triangle, which is prominent near the zenith in the summer months (page 51). Altair and the rest of Aquila are best seen in the early autumn.

ARA
Charts 2, 3, 6; RA 17h dec −50°

ARIES
Chart 5; RA 2h dec 20°; January
Aries is a rather insignificant constellation of the zodiac, and lies south of Andromeda. Its brightest star is the second-magnitude Hamal, which is midway between the Square of Pegasus and Aldebaran, in Taurus. Aries is best placed for observation in the early winter months.

AURIGA
Charts 1, 4, 5; RA 6h dec 40°; January
Auriga's brightest star is the intensely yellow, zero-magnitude Capella – the sixth-brightest star in the sky, and the third-brightest north of the celestial equator. Capella lies midway between

Orion and Polaris; it may also be located by using the stars of the Plough (page 51). Capella and the second-magnitude Menkalinan are circumpolar from the latitude of London. The constellation as a whole is best seen in January. The second-magnitude star Elnath (sometimes spelt Al Nath), which may be considered part of the pattern of Auriga, belongs officially to Taurus, where it marks the tip of one of the bull's horns.

BOÖTES
Charts 1, 3; RA 15h dec 30°; January
Boötes lies to the south-east of Ursa Major. Its leader is the strikingly orange zero-magnitude Arcturus, the brightest star in the northern celestial hemisphere, and the fourth-brightest of all the stars. Arcturus is prominent in the southern sky during the months of summer. Arcturus, and the rest of the constellation, are easily located from the Plough by following the curve of the Plough's 'handle', which continues round to Spica in Virgo (page 51). Boötes also contains the second-magnitude Izar.

CAELUM
Charts 5, 6; RA 5h dec −40°

CAMELOPARDALIS
Charts 1, 5; RA 5h dec 60°

CANCER
Chart 4; RA 9h dec 20°; January
The faintest of the constellations of the zodiac, Cancer is bounded to the west by Castor and Pollux in Gemini, to the east by the Sickle of Leo, and to the south by the little group of stars representing the head of Hydra. Cancer is best placed for observation as winter gives way to spring.

CANES VENATICI
Charts 1, 3; RA 13h dec 40°; January
A small constellation just below the 'handle' of the Plough. Its brightest star, named Cor Caroli, is only of third magnitude, but is easily found as there are no bright stars nearby.

CANIS MAJOR
Chart 4; RA 7h dec −20°; January
A prominent constellation to the south-east of Orion, lying close to the Milky Way. It is dominated by the brilliant white Sirius (sometimes called the Dog Star), at magnitude −1.44 the brightest star in the sky, easily located by continuing the line of the three stars of Orion's belt (page 50). Canis Major is best seen in late January and early February, when its southernmost stars, notably Adhara, Wezen and Aludra, are clear of the horizon as seen from London. With Procyon and Betelgeuse, Sirius makes up what is sometimes called the Winter Triangle.

CANIS MINOR
Chart 4; RA 8h dec 10°; January
A small constellation close to the Milky Way east of Orion, in line with Bellatrix and Betelgeuse. Its brightest star is the pale yellow, first-magnitude Procyon which, with Betelgeuse and Sirius, forms the so-called Winter Triangle. February is the best time to see Canis Minor.

CAPRICORNUS
Chart 2; RA 21h dec −20°; June
A zodiacal constellation south of the celestial equator. Its brightest star, of third magnitude, lies about a third of the way along a line from Fomalhaut in Piscis Austrinus to Altair in Aquila; from there the constellation extends to the west and south-west. Capricornus is highest in the sky in September.

CARINA
Charts 4, 6; RA 6h to 11h, dec −60°
A southern constellation whose brightest star, Canopus, lies midway between Sirius and the south celestial pole. The brilliant pale yellow Canopus, with a magnitude of −0.62, is the second-brightest star in the sky. From Canopus the rest of the constellation extends south-eastward towards the Milky Way. Carina's other bright stars are Avior and Miaplacidus.

CASSIOPEIA
Charts 1, 2, 5; RA 1h dec 60°; January
Cassiopeia's five main stars form a very distinctive group resembling a slightly distorted letter W (or M, according to its orientation) drawn slantwise across the Milky Way, on the opposite side of Polaris from the Plough. The brightest of the five are the second-magnitude stars Schedar and Caph, forming the western end of the W. This circumpolar constellation is overhead in autumn and early winter.

CENTAURUS
Charts 3, 4, 6; RA 13h dec −50°; May
Centaurus is a large southern constellation whose northernmost stars, including the second-magnitude Menkent, rise briefly above the horizon in May for observers at the latitude of London. Its southern boundary lies along the Milky Way, where it all but surrounds the tiny but brilliant Crux. Here lie its two brightest stars, Rigil Kent and Hadar (with the alternative names Toliman and Agena, respectively). The orange-yellow Rigil Kent, also commonly known as Alpha Centauri, is the third-brightest star in the sky, with a magnitude of −0.28, and (with the exception of Proxima Centauri, a faint star visible only in telescopes) is also the closest star to the Earth, after the Sun. The first-magnitude Hadar is a blue-white star.

CEPHEUS
Charts 1, 2; RA 22h, dec 70°; January
A northern circumpolar constellation that occupies the triangular region bounded by Cassiopeia, Polaris and Deneb, in Cygnus. It is highest in the sky in September. The southern part of Cepheus lies on the Milky Way; here are its brightest star, second-magnitude Alderamin, and the famous variable star Delta Cephei (pages 52–53).

CETUS
Charts 2, 5; RA 2h dec −10°; January
A large constellation in the middle of what is often called the 'watery' part of the heavens: a large swathe of the night sky occupied by largely inconspicuous constellations with an aquatic theme. The brightest star in Cetus (the Whale), the second-magnitude Deneb Kaitos, has no nearby rivals and is easy to find. This constellation, best seen in the late autumn, contains the remarkable variable star Mira (pages 52–53). Mira can reach second magnitude, but at its faintest it is well below naked-eye visibility. A special symbol is used for it on the charts.

CHAMAELEON
Chart 6; RA 10h dec −70°

CIRCINUS
Charts 3, 6; RA 15h dec −60°

COLUMBA
Charts 4, 5, 6; RA 6h dec −40°; January
A small southern constellation whose brightest stars, of third magnitude, barely rise above a clear southern horizon at the latitude of London on January nights.

COMA BERENICES
Charts 3, 4; RA 13h dec 20°

CORONA AUSTRALIS
Chart 2; RA 19h dec −40°

CORONA BOREALIS

Chart 3; RA 16h dec 30°; February

A semicircle of stars between Boötes and Hercules, the brightest of which is the second-magnitude Alphekka. Corona Borealis is highest in the sky in midsummer.

CORVUS

Charts 3, 4; RA 12h dec −20°; February

A small quadrilateral of stars to the south-west of Spica, in Virgo. Its brightest stars are of third magnitude. Corvus is best placed for observation in the spring.

CRATER

Charts 3, 4; RA 11h dec −20°

CRUX

Charts 3, 4, 6; RA 12h dec −60°

The smallest of all the constellations, but one of the most distinctive, this far-southern group is popularly known as the Southern Cross. Its longer axis, marked by first-magnitude Acrux and second-magnitude Gacrux, points towards the south celestial pole (page 18). Acrux and first-magnitude Mimosa are distinctly blue. Next to Crux is what appears to be a gap in the Milky Way, devoid of stars: this is the Coalsack, a dark cloud of interstellar dust which blocks the light of stars beyond.

CYGNUS

Charts 1, 2; RA 20h dec 40°; January

Sometimes called the Northern Cross, Cygnus is a striking feature during late summer and autumn when it is directly overhead. The brightest star, Deneb, is circumpolar from the latitude of London and is the most distant of all the first-magnitude stars. With Vega (in Lyra) and Altair (in Aquila), Deneb makes up the Summer Triangle, a familiar landmark of the summer skies (page 51). The long axis of the cross, marked by Deneb, second-magnitude Sadr and third-magnitude Albireo, stretches along the Milky Way. Albireo is a well-known double star, consisting of a third-magnitude yellow star with a fifth-magnitude blue companion (page 51).

DELPHINUS

Chart 2; RA 21h dec 20°; May

Delphinus is one of several small constellations in the region between Cygnus, Aquila and Pegasus, a compact group of fourth-magnitude stars that sparkles at the edge of the Milky Way on a clear night. The stars lie to the north-east of Altair, almost in line with the two lower stars of the Square of Pegasus. Delphinus is best placed for observation in the late summer.

DORADO

Charts 5, 6; RA 5h dec −60°

A small southern constellation, about a third of the way along a line from Canopus, in Carina, to Achernar, in Eridanus. Its most notable feature is the Large Magellanic Cloud, one of two small galaxies in orbit around our own Galaxy, which we see as the Milky Way.

DRACO

Charts 1, 2, 3; RA 16h dec 60°; January

Draco is a circumpolar constellation that winds its way around Ursa Minor. Its brightest star is the second-magnitude Eltanin, one of the four stars marking the head of the dragon, just to the north-west of Vega (in Lyra). From there the constellation snakes towards Cepheus, then back in a curve of stars arcing around Kochab in Ursa Minor, and ending in a line of stars running across the top of the Plough (in Ursa Major). Draco is highest in the sky in midsummer.

EQUULEUS

Chart 2; RA 21h dec 10°

ERIDANUS

Charts 5, 6; RA 4h dec 0° to −60°; January
Eridanus is one of the largest constellations.
Representing a river, it begins just to the
north-west of Rigel, in Orion, from where
it meanders back and forth across the sky
before heading southwards, ending in the
first-magnitude blue-white star Achernar.
Achernar and the southern half of
Eridanus are forever out of view from
the latitude of London. Its northern
reaches are best viewed in the early
winter months.

FORNAX

Chart 5; RA 3h dec −30°

GEMINI

Chart 4; RA 7h dec 20°; January
A bright constellation of the zodiac.
Gemini's two brightest stars represent the
legendary Twins: blue-white Castor is just
below first magnitude, and the brighter,
yellow Pollux is of first magnitude. These
stars are easily found by starting from Orion
(page 50). They are also due north of
Procyon, in Canis Minor; to the north
of them the sky is devoid of bright stars.
The rest of the constellation, containing the
second-magnitude Alhena, lies between
Castor and Pollux and Orion. Gemini is
best seen in February.

GRUS

Chart 2; RA 23h dec −50°; September
A constellation to the immediate south
of Piscis Austrinus. From the latitude of
London its northernmost tip is just visible
under good conditions above the southern
horizon during September. Its brightest
star is the second-magnitude Alnair.

HERCULES

Charts 1, 2, 3; RA 17h dec 30°; January
One of the largest constellations, but
not very conspicuous, Hercules contains
no star above third magnitude; the star

Rasalgethi marks the giant's head.
Hercules lies to the west of Lyra, and is
best seen in the early summer months.

HOROLOGIUM

Charts 5, 6; RA 3h dec −50°

HYDRA

Charts 3, 4; RA 8 to 15h dec −20°; January
The largest of all the constellations,
representing a water snake, but by no
means conspicuous. The creature's head
is marked by a distinctive group of
third- and fourth-magnitude stars due
east of Procyon, in Canis Minor. South-
east of the head is Hydra's brightest star,
the second-magnitude Alphard. The rest
of the constellation snakes eastwards,
finishing up south of Virgo. As a whole,
Hydra is best viewed in the early spring.

HYDRUS

Chart 6; RA 2h dec −70°

INDUS

Chart 2, RA 21h dec –50°

LACERTA

Chart 1; RA 22h dec 50°

LEO

Charts 3, 4; RA 11h dec 10°; January
A prominent constellation of the zodiac,
Leo lies below the Plough (page 51),
and midway between the bright stars
Arcturus, in Boötes, and Procyon, in
Canis Minor. Its main feature is the
distinctive Sickle asterism, resembling a
reversed question mark. The 'dot' of the
question mark is Leo's brightest star,
the blue-white, first-magnitude Regulus.
The Sickle also contains the second-
magnitude Algieba. To the east of the
Sickle is a triangle of stars, including
second-magnitude Denebola. Leo is
highest in the sky and best placed for
observation in April.

LEO MINOR
Chart 4; RA 10h dec 30°

LEPUS
Chart 5; RA 5h dec −20°; January
A small group of stars immediately below the 'feet' of Orion, none brighter than third magnitude. Lepus is best placed for viewing in January.

LIBRA
Chart 3; RA 15h dec −20°; April
A constellation of the zodiac located between Scorpius and Virgo; none of its stars is brighter than third magnitude. The best time for viewing Libra is midsummer.

LUPUS
Charts 3, 6; RA 15h dec −40°
A southern constellation to the south-west of Scorpius, running along the edge of the Milky Way. The brightest star is of second magnitude, but Lupus is quite conspicuous on a clear night as it contains quite a high concentration of stars of third and fourth magnitude. From the latitude of London its northernmost members are visible just above the horizon in June.

LYNX
Charts 1, 4; RA 8h dec 50°

LYRA
Charts 1, 2; RA 19h dec 40°; February
Lyra lies just off the northern Milky Way. At magnitude zero, its brightest star, Vega, is the second-brightest in the northern hemisphere, and the fifth-brightest in the whole sky. The brilliant blue-white Vega is prominent near the zenith on summer nights. With Deneb, in Cygnus, and Altair, in Aquila, it makes up the Summer Triangle (page 51), prominent overhead in the summer months. From the latitude of London, Vega is just circumpolar.

MENSA
Chart 6; RA 6h dec −80°
The faintest of all the constellations, located near the south celestial pole. Its only distinction is that it contains part of the Large Magellanic Cloud, one of two small galaxies in orbit around our own Galaxy, which we see as the Milky Way.

MICROSCOPIUM
Chart 2; RA 21h dec −40°

MONOCEROS
Chart 4; RA 7h dec 0°

MUSCA
Chart 6; RA 13h dec −70°

NORMA
Charts 3, 6; RA 16h dec −50°

OCTANS
Chart 6; RA 20h dec −80°
This otherwise unremarkable constellation contains the south celestial pole.

OPHIUCHUS
Chart 3; RA 17h dec −10°; April
A large but not prominent constellation which crosses the celestial equator and lies between Hercules and Scorpius. Although it is not one of the 12 constellations of the traditional zodiac, the ecliptic does pass through it, so planets are sometimes found here. The brightest stars are second-magnitude Rasalhague and Sabik. July is the best time to see Ophiuchus.

ORION
Charts 4, 5; RA 6h dec 0°; January
The most brilliant of all the constellations – an unmistakable feature of the winter skies and the chief guide to the other constellations on view in the winter months (page 50). Rigel's pale blue radiance is set off by the striking

red of Betelgeuse (occasionally spelt Betelgeux); these two first-magnitude stars lie at opposite corners of the constellation's main rectangular pattern. The other two corners are formed by second-magnitude Bellatrix and Saiph. At the centre of the rectangle are the three stars that comprise what is known as Orion's Belt: Alnitak, Alnilam and Mintaka, all of second magnitude. Mintaka lies very close to the celestial equator. Below the Belt is the Orion Nebula, a vast cloud of gas and dust visible to the naked eye as a faint, misty patch (pages 54–55). The constellation is highest in the sky in January.

PAVO

Charts 2, 6; RA 20h dec −70°

A southern constellation lying between Sagittarius and the south celestial pole, whose brightest star, known as Peacock, is of second magnitude.

PEGASUS

Charts 2, 5, RA 23h dec 20°, January

A large constellation best known for the Square of Pegasus: four stars that make up a near-perfect square which is a feature of the skies of late summer, autumn and early winter. The Square, which is on the opposite side of Cassiopeia from Polaris, itself provides a useful means of locating other constellations (page 50). The four stars of the square are Alpheratz (which officially belongs to Andromeda), Scheat, Markab and Algenib, all second magnitude apart from Algenib, which is third magnitude. From the Square, the rest of the constellation, including second-magnitude Enif, extends to the west towards the Summer Triangle (page 51). A line traced from Algenib to Polaris (passing first through Alpheratz and then Caph, in Cassiopeia) roughly indicates the zero line from which right ascension is measured.

PERSEUS

Charts 1, 5; RA 4h dec 40°; January

Perseus lies to the south of a line between Cassiopeia and Capella, in Auriga, and north of the Pleiades, in Taurus. Most of the constellation is circumpolar for observers at the latitude of London. Second-magnitude Mirfak is the brightest star, and Algol is a well-known variable star, fluctuating between second and fourth magnitude. Perseus lies on the Milky Way, and on a clear night is conspicuous with its sprinkling of third- and fourth-magnitude stars. It is highest in the sky at the end of the year.

PHOENIX

Charts 2, 5; RA 1h dec −50°

A southern constellation that lies between Achernar, in Eridanus, and Fomalhaut, in Piscis Austrinus. Its brightest star is the second-magnitude Ankaa.

PICTOR

Charts 4, 5, 6; RA 6h dec −60°

PISCES

Charts 2, 5; RA 1h dec 10°; January

Pisces is a large constellation, one of the 12 that make up the zodiac, but is quite inconspicuous, containing no star brighter than fourth magnitude. It occupies the area to the east and south of the Square of Pegasus, in the 'watery' region of the sky: Cetus (the Whale) lies to its south, and Aquarius to the west. Pisces is best seen in November.

PISCIS AUSTRINUS

Chart 2; RA 22h dec −30°; August

A constellation whose brightest star, Fomalhaut, is located by dropping a line southwards from the western edge of the square of Pegasus (page 50). Fomalhaut is visible for a short time in the autumn when the horizon is clear; there are no bright stars close to it.

PUPPIS

Charts 4, 6; RA 8h dec −40°; January

Puppis occupies the region between and to the east of Canis Major and Canopus, in Carina, extending towards the Milky Way. Its northernmost stars are visible from the latitude of London in the late winter months, to the east of Aludra, in Canis Minor.

PYXIS

Chart 4; RA 9h dec −30°

RETICULUM

Charts 5, 6; RA 4h dec −60°

SAGITTA

Chart 2; RA 20h dec 20°; May

A faint but distinctive arrow-shaped formation of stars in the Milky Way just north of Altair, in Aquila. Sagitta is highest in the sky in the late summer.

SAGITTARIUS

Charts 2, 3; RA 19h dec −30°; June

A bright constellation of the zodiac, situated in the Milky Way to the east of Scorpius and south of Aquila. Its northern part contains its brightest stars, including the second-magnitude Nunki and Kaus Australis, and is visible in the summer low on the southern horizon. The fainter, southern portion never rises above the horizon of observers at the latitude of London.

SCORPIUS

Charts 3, 6; RA 17h dec −30°; May

A conspicuous and distinctively shaped constellation of the zodiac, lying in the Milky Way to the west of Sagittarius. Like its neighbour Sagittarius, only its northern section is visible from the latitude of London. This part, which contains the constellation's brightest stars, orange-red first-magnitude Antares, and Graffias, just below second magnitude, is best seen in midsummer. The southern stars,

making up the scorpion's sting, include Shaula, one of the brightest of all second-magnitude stars.

SCULPTOR

Charts 2, 5; RA 0h dec −30°

SCUTUM

Chart 2; RA 19h dec −10°

SERPENS

Charts 2, 3; RA 18h dec −10° (Cauda)
RA 16h 10° (Caput); March

This constellation has the distinction of being the only one that is split into two sections. The western part, between Ophiuchus and Arcturus, in Boötes, represents the serpent's head and is often referred to as Serpens Caput. Its tail, Serpens Cauda, lies between Ophiuchus and Aquila. Its brightest stars are of third magnitude. Serpens is best viewed in the summer months.

SEXTANS

Chart 4; RA 10h dec 0°

TAURUS

Chart 5; RA 4h dec 20°; January

A prominent constellation of the zodiac, lying between Orion and Perseus, just off the Milky Way. Its brightest star is the first-magnitude, orange-red Aldebaran, found by following the line of Orion's Belt to the north. The second-brightest is Elnath, midway between Betelgeuse, in Orion, and Capella, in Auriga. The line from Orion's Belt to Aldebaran continues to the Pleiades, a prominent star cluster with six members visible to the naked eye, more on clear nights (page 54). Behind Aldebaran is another star cluster, the Hyades (page 54), whose members are rather more scattered; the brightest form a distinctive V shape. Taurus is highest in the sky and best placed for observation in December.

TELESCOPIUM
Chart 2; RA 19h dec −50°

TRIANGULUM
Chart 5; RA 2h dec 30; January
A small constellation just to the south-east of Almaak and Mirach, in Andromeda. Its brightest stars are of third magnitude. Triangulum is best seen at the end of November.

TRIANGULUM AUSTRALE
Chart 6; RA 16h dec −70°
A southern constellation in the Milky Way to the south-east of Rigil Kent, in Centaurus, and rather more prominent than its northern namesake. Its brightest star, of second magnitude, is known as Atria.

TUCANA
Chart 2, 5; RA 23h dec −60°
A southern constellation, found between Achernar, in Eridanus, and Peacock, in Pavo. Its brightest star is of third magnitude. Tucana contains the Small Magellanic Cloud, one of two small galaxies in orbit around our own Galaxy, which we see as the Milky Way.

URSA MAJOR
Charts 1, 3, 4; RA 12h dec 50°; January
Seven of the brightest stars of this large constellation together form the asterism known as the Plough or Big Dipper, the most familiar pattern of the northern sky. They are, from west to east, Dubhe, Merak, Phad, Megrez, Alioth, Mizar and Alkaid, all of second magnitude except for Megrez, which is third magnitude. The Plough is circumpolar from the latitude of London, and is an important aid to locating other constellations in the region (page 51). Dubhe and Merak are known as the Pointers – a line through them leads to Polaris, providing the best way of finding direction at night. Very close to Mizar is a fainter star, Alcor; the two are not physically related, happening to lie on almost the same line of sight. Ursa Major is the third-largest constellation. Its other stars extend to the west and south, in the direction of Leo. The best time of year to see the whole constellation is in April.

URSA MINOR
Chart 1; RA 16h dec 80°; January
Ursa Minor contains the north celestial pole, marked by second-magnitude Polaris. Like all other stars, Polaris actually revolves around the pole, but it is so close to the pole that its motion is negligible and it can be taken as marking true north at all times. The other bright star in Ursa Minor, also of second magnitude, is Kochab.

VELA
Charts 4, 6; RA 9h dec −50°
A southern constellation, lying on the Milky Way to the north of Carina.

VIRGO
Charts 3, 4; RA 13h dec 0°; January
The second-largest of the constellations, Virgo lies on the celestial equator and is one of the 12 star groups of the zodiac. Its brightest star, the blue first-magnitude Spica, is found by tracing the curve of the Plough's handle, to Arcturus, and continuing a similar distance. Arcturus, Spica and Denebola, in Leo, make up an almost equilateral triangle. From Spica, the constellation extends to the west towards Leo and to the east in the direction of Serpens and Libra. Virgo is best placed for observation in the spring.

VOLANS
Chart 6; RA 8h dec −70°

VULPECULA
Chart 2; RA 20h dec 20°